Vivo V30 Series

A Sneak Peek into the Zeiss-Powered Flagships

David Wilson

Vivo V30 Series

Table of Contents

Vivo V30 Series

Introduction

The Excitement Surrounding the Vivo V30 Series Launch

Businesses in the smartphone sector are continuously pushing the envelope of innovation in an effort to draw in customers. One such business, Vivo, is well-known for its innovative technologies and stylish looks, and it has been making waves lately. There is a tangible sense of excitement among fans waiting for the presentation of the new flagship devices that will make up the Vivo V30 series.

Zeiss optics' incorporation into the Vivo V30 series is one of the main things generating the buzz. Zeiss is known for producing high-quality lenses and imaging solutions, and the company's partnership with Vivo is a major turning point for the smartphone market.

Both tech geeks and smartphone photographers are excited to see how this collaboration will improve the smartphone photography experience, especially with Zeiss optics promised for the Vivo V30 series.

With its outstanding array of features and capabilities, the Vivo V30 series is expected to build upon the success of its predecessors. These smartphones are ready to raise the bar for smartphone performance and innovation thanks to their potent processors, gorgeous displays, and sophisticated camera systems. Customer excitement is building as the launch date draws near, and they can't wait to get their hands on these much-anticipated products.

We'll look at what's causing the hype around the launch of the Vivo V30 series and what to expect from the inclusion of Zeiss optics in this introduction.

We will explore the significance of this partnership and talk about what the forthcoming flagship smartphones will have in store for customers. We'll also discuss the anticipated effects of the Vivo V30 series on the smartphone market and the larger tech sector overall. In summary, this overview prepares readers for a closer look at the Vivo V30 series and how it might completely change the smartphone market.

Awaiting the Integration of Zeiss Optics

A major advancement in smartphone photography technology is represented by the Vivo V30 series' incorporation of Zeiss optics. With a long history of creating premium lenses for cameras and other optical devices, Zeiss is well-known for its proficiency in optical engineering and imaging solutions. Vivo hopes to use this knowledge to give its clients the best possible photography experience by collaborating with Zeiss.

Zeiss optics are projected to substantially enhance the quality of the Vivo V30 series' camera system, which is one of its most anticipated features.

Zeiss lenses are renowned for their remarkable sharpness, clarity, and color reproduction, which enable users to take breathtaking pictures and films with astonishing precision and detail. The Zeiss-powered camera system of the Vivo V30 series makes it capable of producing exceptional results whether it is used to capture stunning vistas, vivid portraits, or quick action photos.

Beyond hardware, the Vivo V30 series benefits from improved image algorithms and software optimizations thanks to the integration of Zeiss optics. These improvements are intended to improve photography even further by making it easier for users to take pictures of high quality. The Vivo V30 series is anticipated to provide a wide range of capabilities that will satisfy the needs of both casual users and photography aficionados, from sophisticated picture stabilization and low-light performance to intelligent scene recognition.

Apart from photography, other areas of the smartphone experience, such videography and augmented reality (AR) applications, are anticipated to gain from the incorporation of Zeiss optics. Because of their reputation for adaptability and versatility, Zeiss lenses are excellent choices for a variety of creative endeavors. The Vivo V30 series is ready to enable users to unleash their creativity and express themselves in novel and exciting ways, whether it's by capturing cinematic video footage, producing immersive augmented reality experiences, or investigating new avenues in mobile photography.

All things considered, the excitement around the inclusion of Zeiss optics into the Vivo V30 series is indicative of the growing need for creative smartphone photography solutions. It is impossible to overestimate the significance of high-quality camera technology, as customers increasingly depend on their smartphones to record and share special experiences. The Vivo V30 series, with Zeiss optics at the forefront, is ready to raise the bar for smartphone photography and establish new benchmarks for image technology excellence.

Chapter 1: Teasing the Vivo V30 and V30 Pro

The official teases and listings for the Vivo V30 and V30 Pro have been providing enticing views of what's to come, thus the excitement for their introduction has been slowly growing. Vivo has been building excitement by revealing the elegant design of its next flagship smartphones and teasing important hardware specifications, as smartphone aficionados anxiously anticipate the announcement of these new products.

Official Listings and Teasers

Vivo has been using a variety of platforms, including as its official website and social media accounts, to carefully tease the release of the V30 and V30 Pro. Through creating talk about the upcoming devices and piqueing customer interest, these teasers help to build anticipation for their formal unveiling.

Vivo's teaser campaign is noteworthy for emphasizing important features and advancements that differentiate the V30 and V30 Pro from their predecessors. With their cutting-edge camera technology and potent performance capabilities, these teasers offer a sneak peek at the fascinating new features that owners of the newest Vivo phones may anticipate.

Vivo has added official teasers to its website, where customers can examine the features and specifications of the upcoming V30 and V30 Pro in greater depth. These listings help customers make educated decisions about their future smartphone purchase by offering useful details on the hardware and software capabilities of the V30 and V30 Pro.

Design Revelations and Essential Hardware Information

The focus on design in Vivo's teaser campaign is one of its most intriguing features, as the company highlights the svelte and fashionable looks of the V30 and V30 Pro. These gadgets stand out from the competition thanks to their sophisticated and elegant designs, which include curved screens and thin bezels.

Along with the design, Vivo has been leaking important hardware information about the future V30 and V30 Pro, emphasizing the potent processors, gorgeous displays, and cutting-edge camera systems that will be present in the handsets. Vivo's dedication to provide cutting-edge technology and performance in its flagship smartphones, guaranteeing that customers have access to the newest and finest features, is emphasized by these hardware specifics.

All things considered, Vivo's teaser campaign for the V30 and V30 Pro has been successful in building consumer enthusiasm and anticipation. Vivo has successfully created anticipation for the impending release of its flagship smartphones by subtly revealing important features and breakthroughs, highlighting the elegant look of the handsets, and offering insightful details about their technical capabilities. Customers are excited to see how the V30 and V30 Pro will change the smartphone landscape and are anxious to get their hands on them when the launch date draws near.

Chapter 2: Unveiling the Vivo V30 Pro with Zeiss Optics

As the first smartphone in the V-series lineup to debut with Zeiss optics, the Vivo V30 Pro's release represents a significant milestone for the lineup. The Vivo V30 Pro is expected to bring advanced technologies and an improved photographic experience, building on the popularity of its predecessor, the Vivo V29 series. Let's examine this much awaited device's specifications and see how it seeks to revolutionize smartphone photography.

Debuting as the First V-Series Phone with Zeiss Optics

The Vivo V30 Pro is distinguished by its collaboration with Zeiss, a well-known optical brand recognized for its superior lenses and image products. Vivo's dedication to providing best-in-class camera performance is demonstrated by this partnership, which is the first time Zeiss optics have been integrated into a V-series smartphone.

Users benefit from improved image quality, increased clarity, and excellent low-light performance thanks to the inclusion of Zeiss optics into the V30 Pro. Zeiss lenses are well known for their exquisite engineering and capacity to capture exquisite detail, which makes them the ideal match for Vivo's cutting edge camera technology.

Users may anticipate crisper, more vivid images with true-to-life colors and remarkable dynamic range when Zeiss optics are included. The V30 Pro is designed to provide images of a caliber that can compete with dedicated cameras, whether it is shooting low-light scenarios, landscapes, or portraits.

Beyond image quality, Vivo's dedication to innovation and pushing the limits of smartphone photography is further demonstrated by its cooperation with Zeiss. Vivo hopes to redefine mobile imagery and enable consumers to express their creativity by utilizing Zeiss's experience and state-of-the-art technology.

Successor to the Vivo V29 Lineup

As the V29 lineup's replacement, the Vivo V30 Pro builds on its predecessor's popularity by bringing about a number of significant upgrades and refinements. The sleek appearance, robust performance, and adaptable camera system of the V29 series were highly praised; nevertheless, the V30 Pro seeks to enhance these attributes even further.

Because Zeiss optics are integrated, one area in which the V30 Pro shines is its camera capabilities. The V30 Pro promises to provide unmatched image quality and versatility by utilizing Zeiss's experience in lens design and optical technology. The V30 Pro's camera system delivers outstanding results whether taking crisp images, capturing fluid videos, or experimenting with artistic effects.

The V30 Pro is not only a powerful performer with the newest processors, lots of RAM and storage, and a bright display, but it also has imaging capabilities.

These features make it possible for users to be productive and engaged while on the go by ensuring seamless multitasking, immersive gaming, and a seamless user experience.

Ultimately, the Vivo V30 Pro is the next step forward for the V-series lineup, bringing together cutting-edge technology, gorgeous design, and unique photography functions to create a smartphone that is simply remarkable. The V30 Pro is positioned to revolutionize smartphone photography and establish new benchmarks for photographic quality with its launch as the first phone in the V-series to include Zeiss optics.

Chapter 3: Confirmation of India Launch and Flipkart Availability

Smartphone lovers are excited by the announcement of the Vivo V30 series' India launch and availability on Flipkart, as hype surrounding the device has been growing. Let's examine the specifics around the launch confirmation and Flipkart availability of the Vivo V30 and V30 Pro as Vivo gets ready to introduce its newest products to the Indian market.

Listing on Vivo's Website and Flipkart

The official inclusion of the Vivo V30 and V30 Pro on Flipkart and the Vivo website is evidence of the company's dedication to the Indian market. Customers may make educated selections about what to buy by using these listings, which give them vital details about the gadgets, such as features, costs, availability, and specifications.

Users may view comprehensive product pages for the V30 and V30 Pro on Vivo's website, which highlight the devices' features, performance, and other important aspects. These sections are a thorough resource for prospective customers, providing information about what Vivo's most recent products have to offer.

Like the Vivo V30 series, Flipkart has also made specific landing pages that emphasize the smartphones' salient features and provide customers the chance to express interest or place a preorder. Vivo V30 series exposure and accessibility are further enhanced by Flipkart's wide reach and user-friendly UI, which make it a favorite platform for many Indian buyers.

Availability of Vivo V30 and V30 Pro in India

An exciting chance for customers to experience the newest advancements in smartphone technology has been confirmed with the launch of the Vivo V30 series in India. India, one of the biggest smartphone markets in the world, is very important to Vivo, and the company's choice to launch the V30 series there demonstrates its belief in the market's potential.

Customers can anticipate obtaining cutting-edge gadgets with outstanding performance, gorgeous designs, and sophisticated camera functions when the Vivo V30 and V30 Pro make their debut in India. The V30 series is designed to meet the demands and tastes of a diverse variety of users, including those who are passionate about productivity, mobile gaming, or photography.

Additionally, Flipkart's availability of the Vivo V30 and V30 Pro guarantees broad accessibility throughout India, enabling customers from different areas to easily buy the handsets online.

Flipkart's dependable delivery services and strong logistics network further expedite the buying procedure, guaranteeing a flawless shopping experience for clients.

In conclusion, the announcement of the Vivo V30 series' launch in India and its availability on Flipkart signals the start of an exciting new phase in Vivo's development as a smartphone manufacturer in India. The V30 series is set to create a big impression and win over discriminating Indian consumers looking for the newest and best smartphone technology thanks to its cutting-edge features, fashionable design, and affordable price.

Chapter 4: Key Specifications and Features

Important features and specs are vital in the highly competitive smartphone market when it comes to a device's consumer appeal. Vivo hopes to satisfy smartphone consumers' varied wants and tastes with the Vivo V30 series, which has an amazing assortment of features and specifications. The main features and specifications of the Vivo V30 and V30 Pro are covered in detail in this chapter, with particular attention paid to the processor, display, camera configuration, battery life, and other important details.

Camera Setup, Processor, and Display Configuration

The strong processing unit that powers the Vivo V30 series' smooth performance and multitasking abilities is at its core. The most recent Qualcomm Snapdragon processors included in the devices provide lag-free performance and effective power management. The V30 series offers snappy performance and increased efficiency whether customers are streaming movies, gaming, or using many programs at once.

Vivo has made no compromises when it comes to display quality to give customers engaging viewing experiences. The remarkable OLED screens of the V30 and

V30 Pro boast sharp details, rich blacks, and vivid colors. The displays are perfect for gaming, multimedia consumption, and office tasks since they have high refresh rates and support for HDR, which provide fluid animations and lifelike graphics.

The excellent camera system of the Vivo V30 series is one of its best characteristics; it's made to take beautiful pictures and videos in any situation. With an amazing selection of camera lenses, including ultra-wide, telephoto, and macro lenses, the V30 Pro, which draws on the expertise of Zeiss optics, allows users to easily create stunning photos and unleash their creativity.

In addition, the V30 series features state-of-the-art camera technologies that guarantee outstanding image quality in a variety of lighting scenarios, including AI scene recognition, night mode, and sophisticated image processing algorithms. Users can anticipate unmatched clarity, detail, and color accuracy from the V30 series cameras, whether they are shooting close-ups, landscapes, or portraits.

Battery Capacity and Other Notable Specs

For smartphone users, especially those who are always on the go, battery life is just as important as performance and image capabilities. With strong battery capacities that guarantee extended use on a single charge, the Vivo V30 series allays this worry. The extended uptime provided by the V30 and V30 Pro's big battery units and clever power management technologies enables users to remain connected and productive all day.

A number of other noteworthy features that improve the user experience overall are also included in the Vivo V30 series. These include the newest networking standards, such 5G compatibility, which provide flawless connectivity and fast data transfer speeds, expandable storage options, enhanced security features like facial recognition and in-display fingerprint sensors, and rapid charging support.

Finally, because of its remarkable range of features and characteristics, the Vivo V30 series stands out as a strong competitor in the smartphone market. The V30 series offers a compelling combination that meets the demands of contemporary smartphone consumers, with features including improved camera systems, long-lasting battery life, and strong processors and gorgeous displays. The V30 series is a great option for discriminating customers looking for a high-end smartphone experience since it offers remarkable performance and versatility, whether used for work, play, or creative endeavors.

Chapter 5: Competitors and Pricing Expectations

Manufacturer competition in the ever-changing smartphone industry is intense, with each brand striving to provide consumers with the most alluring features and value proposition. Evaluating these smartphones' relative merits to rival models from other manufacturers is crucial as Vivo gets ready to introduce the V30 series. Furthermore, for buyers wishing to make well-informed selections, it is essential to comprehend the Vivo V30 series' expected price and release date. This chapter delves into the rivals of the Vivo V30 series, looking at their anticipated costs and release schedules.

Comparison with Rival Models

Numerous options, catering to distinct customer niches, are available in the smartphone industry, ranging from flagship smartphones to mid-range products. A number of aspects are taken into consideration when comparing the Vivo V30 series to its rivals, including features, design, specifications, and overall value.

The OnePlus Nord 3, with a comparable target market and price range, is one of the main rivals of the Vivo V30 series. Both gadgets are attractive options for customers looking for premium features at a reasonable price since they include strong processors, bright displays, and adaptable camera setups. But the Zeiss optics integration that sets the Vivo V30 series apart from the competition allows for better imaging performance.

The Xiaomi Redmi Note 13 Pro, which provides impressive features and specifications at an appealing price point, is another competitor in the mid-range market. The Redmi Note 13 Pro is still a well-liked option among users who value value for money above price, even though it may not have some of the high-end features of the Vivo V30 series, such as Zeiss optics and sophisticated camera technologies.

The Vivo V30 series faces stiff competition in the flagship market from the Samsung Galaxy S24 Ultra, which offers state-of-the-art features, an elegant design, and a wide range of services and accessories. Even though the Galaxy S24 Ultra costs more than the V30 series, it appeals to discriminating buyers looking for the best smartphone experience because it has a wide range of features and capabilities.

Expected Pricing and Release Date

The Vivo V30 series is much anticipated by users, and there is a lot of conjecture about the devices' debut timing and price. Analysts and industry insiders provide information about what users might anticipate in terms of availability and cost, even though Vivo has not yet officially verified any facts.

The Vivo V30 series' features and positioning lead one to believe that the smartphones will be affordably priced to appeal to a wide range of users. Vivo has historically used aggressive pricing techniques, therefore it's probable that the V30 series will provide exceptional value for money when compared to its rivals in the mid-range and flagship markets.

According to Vivo, the V30 series will make its Indian debut on February 28 and become available on Flipkart and other retail channels shortly after. Vivo's approach of introducing its smartphones in strategic worldwide regions to harness customer demand and optimize sales potential is in line with this.

In conclusion, in the congested smartphone industry, competitor manufacturers present serious competition for the Vivo V30 series. But the V30 series is set to make a big impression and carve out a position for itself among customers looking for high-end smartphones thanks to its intriguing specs, cutting-edge features, and affordable price. Expectations are high as the launch date draws near, and customers can't wait to see how the Vivo V30 series compares to its rivals and experience it for themselves.

Conclusion

It's clear that the Vivo V30 series of smartphones is expected to have a big impact on the smartphone market as excitement for its release grows. The V30 series promises to give an amazing user experience and meet the wide range of needs of consumers with a plethora of innovative features. We provide a summary of the expected features and significance of the Vivo V30 series in this conclusion, along with some final observations on its impending release.

An Overview of Expected Features and Their Impact

It is anticipated that the Vivo V30 series will include a number of noteworthy characteristics that distinguish it from its rivals. One of the standout features is the use of Zeiss optics, which is a first for a V-series phone in terms of sophisticated camera technology. Vivo's dedication to provide best-in-class image capabilities and elevating the standard for smartphone photography is demonstrated by its relationship with Zeiss.

Apart from its exceptional photography capabilities, the Vivo V30 series is anticipated to astound customers with its potent performance, courtesy of the most recent Qualcomm Snapdragon processors and ample RAM setups. Smooth and responsive performance is expected from the V30 series, regardless of the task—multitasking, gaming, or productivity.

It is also expected that the V30 series would have breathtaking displays with vivid colors, fast refresh rates, and engaging viewing experiences. The visual accuracy and clarity of the V30 series displays are sure to enthrall and satisfy customers whether they're playing games, viewing movies, or browsing the web.

The Vivo V30 series is also anticipated to perform very well in the area of battery life, thanks to its big capacity batteries and effective power management that guarantee longer usage periods between charges. For consumers leading busy lives, the V30 series is expected to deliver dependable battery life, regardless of whether they are working on heavy tasks or traveling.

Final Thoughts on the Launch of the Vivo V30 Series

Customers and industry analysts alike are exhibiting a strong sense of enthusiasm and expectation as the Vivo V30 series launch date approaches. The V30 series, which highlights Vivo's dedication to quality, innovation, and user experience, marks an important turning point for the firm.

The Vivo V30 series boasts a sleek appearance, affordable pricing, and state-of-the-art capabilities that make it appealing to a broad spectrum of customers, including mainstream users and tech enthusiasts. The V30 series offers something for everyone, whether it's the appeal of premium design, the promise of powerful performance, or the allure of Zeiss optics.

To sum up, the debut of the Vivo V30 series is expected to be a momentous occasion that will reshape the smartphone industry and establish new standards for quality. Vivo is prepared to fulfill its promise of innovation, performance, and quality as customers anxiously await the chance to have the V30 series in their hands, solidifying its place as a major force in the worldwide smartphone market.